MY PET
Rabbit

Honor Head

Photographs by
Jane Burton

RAINTREE
STECK-VAUGHN
PUBLISHERS

A Harcourt Company

Austin   New York
www.steck-vaughn.com

Published by Raintree Steck-Vaughn
Publishers, an imprint of Steck-Vaughn
Company.

Editors: Claire Edwards, Erik Greb
Art Director: Max Brinkmann
Illustrator: Pauline Bayne
Designer: Rosamund Saunders

Printed in Singapore

1 2 3 4 5 6 7 8 9 0 LB 03 02 01 00

**Library of Congress Cataloging-in-Publication
Data**

Head, Honor.
  Rabbit/Honor Head; photographs by Jane Burton.
    p. cm.—(My pet)
  Summary: Describes the physical characteristics
and habits of rabbits and tells how to care for
them as pets.
  ISBN 0-7398-2887-8 (hardcover)
  ISBN 0-7398-3013-9 (softcover)
  1. Rabbits—Juvenile literature. [1. Rabbits.
2. Animals—Infancy. 3. Pets.] I. Burton, Jane, ill.
II. Title.

SF453.2 H43 2000
                    00–027053

Contents

My Rabbit

ears

nose

paws

fur

claws

It's fun to have your own pet.

Rabbits look very sweet and are fun to have as pets, but they need to be looked after carefully.

A rabbit needs to be fed every day. You will have to clean out its hutch and make sure that it is happy and healthy. Most of all, remember that your rabbit may be with you for many years.

Young children with pets should always work with an adult. For further notes, please see page 32.

There are many different types of rabbits.

Some rabbits have long, fluffy fur. They look very soft, but they need to be groomed every day.

A big rabbit may be too heavy for you to pick up when it is fully grown. They need lots of space and eat more than smaller rabbits.

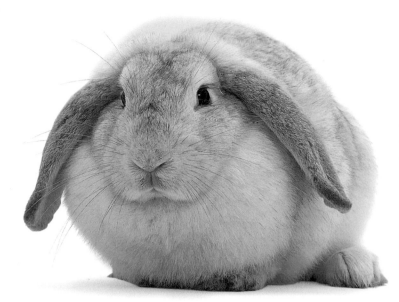

Lop-eared rabbits have long, droopy ears. You have to be careful to keep their ears clean.

Some rabbits are bred specially for their markings, such as spots and patches. Some have colored ears, faces, and feet.

This rabbit is a dwarf rabbit. Small rabbits are easier to pick up and will not eat as much as big rabbits.

When baby rabbits are born, they are helpless.

When a rabbit is pregnant, she uses fur from her tummy to make a soft nest for her babies.

A mother rabbit does not look pregnant until about a week before the babies are born. Give her more food and drink, but do not touch her.

Rabbits usually have about five babies, but some rabbits may have as many as ten babies.

Newborn rabbits do not have any fur. They cannot see or hear. Do not touch them until they are at least three weeks old.

Rabbits grow very quickly.

When baby rabbits are very small, do not pick them up or touch them.

When the rabbit is three weeks old, it has all its fur. Its eyes are wide open. Now it can run and jump around.

Rabbits' fur shows at four days. Their eyes open at about one week.

Baby rabbits find their way to
their mother's milk by smell.
Drinking their mother's milk is
called suckling.

A rabbit is old enough to
leave its mother when it is
about eight weeks old.

Your rabbit needs a cozy place to live.

Have a hutch ready for your new pet. The hutch should have two parts, one you can see into and one where the rabbit can sleep.

Your rabbit will also need a water bottle and a food bowl.

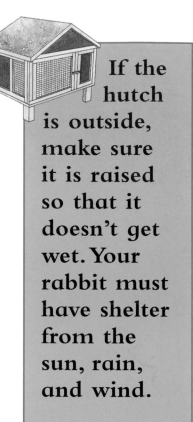

If the hutch is outside, make sure it is raised so that it doesn't get wet. Your rabbit must have shelter from the sun, rain, and wind.

Cover the floor of the hutch with newspaper and sawdust or wood shavings. Put in lots of hay where the rabbit will sleep.

Put a large wire pen (called a run) in the backyard for your rabbit. Move it from time to time so that your rabbit has fresh grass to eat.

Your rabbit will like to be held.

Your rabbit may be scared of you at first.
Let it smell your hand. Then, leave it in its
hutch for a day before you pick it up.
Then, stroke the rabbit gently, so that it
grows used to you.

Talk quietly to your
rabbit so that it gets used
to the sound of your
voice. Stroke it in the
same direction that
its fur grows.

14

Sit or kneel to pick up your rabbit. Place one hand under its chest, behind its front legs. Use your other hand to scoop up its bottom. Never squeeze your rabbit or pick it up by its ears.

If your rabbit struggles, put it down gently. Place its back legs on the floor first. Never drop your rabbit or you will hurt it.

You can train your rabbit.

If you let your rabbit run around indoors, train it to use a litter box. Watch where it goes to the toilet and leave the litter box there.

Empty the litter box every day. Wash it with warm water and pet germ killer once a week. Wear rubber gloves when cleaning your rabbit's box.

If your rabbit does something it shouldn't, such as trying to kick you, say "No." Do not hit your rabbit. When it stops being naughty, give it something to eat.

Train your rabbit to come to you. Kneel on the ground and hold out a piece of food. Wait for your rabbit to come to the food. Never chase your rabbit.

Your rabbit likes to eat at regular times.

Give your rabbit a morning meal of special rabbit mix. In the evening give it some vegetables and fruit, such as apples, cabbage, or carrots.

Put the food in a heavy bowl, or your rabbit may knock it over. Always wash fresh food and cut it into small chunks. Take away any stale, or old, food.

Make sure your rabbit has enough water. Buy a special water bottle. Make sure it is always filled with fresh water.

Your rabbit should have lots of hay to munch during the day.

Rabbits also enjoy parsnips and celery. If you can, pick some clover or dandelion leaves for your pet.

Keep your rabbit's hutch clean.

Clear away your rabbit's droppings and any wet wood shavings every day.

Clean the hutch once a week—more often when the weather is hot. Throw away old bedding and sweep out the hutch. Put in clean sawdust and bedding.

Every two weeks give the hutch a real cleaning. Put your rabbit in a safe place. Rinse the hutch with soapy water. Then, spray it with a germ-killing spray from a pet store.

Wash out your rabbit's water bottle at least once a week. Use a bottle brush, which you can buy from a pet store.

Your rabbit will want to play.

Your rabbit will need plenty of exercise. It will enjoy exploring in the backyard or indoors.

If your rabbit is running around indoors, keep the doors and windows shut. Always stay in the room with your rabbit when it is exploring.

Rabbits are very curious. Leave out boxes or baskets for your pet to explore.

Don't let your rabbit chew any wires or cables. Make sure sharp things, such as scissors or pins, are out of reach.

Make sure your rabbit is healthy.

Most rabbits keep their
own fur clean and healthy.
But they also like to
be brushed.

Use a soft brush and brush your
pet from its head down to its
tail. Gently stroke underneath
your rabbit's body to
remove any bedding
caught in its fur.

Your rabbit will need a mineral block to chew. This will help to keep your pet healthy.

Give your rabbit a log or a wooden block to gnaw on. Gnawing this will keep its teeth from growing too long.

Look at your rabbit carefully every day. If your rabbit has dull fur, runny eyes, nose or ears, or has diarrhea, take it to the vet as soon as possible.

25

Your rabbit will want a friend.

In the wild, rabbits live in groups, so your rabbit will enjoy having a friend. Female rabbits from the same litter make a perfect pair.

Rabbits get along well with guinea pigs if they meet when they are both young. Make sure they have enough space in the hutch.

Do not put a
female rabbit with
a male that has not
been neutered. They
will have lots of
babies and you will
not be able to look
after them.

Rabbits and cats or
dogs can get along
together if they meet
when they are both
very young.
Usually you should
keep cats and dogs
away from your rabbit.

Rabbits can live for eight years or more.

Rabbits can live for up to about
12 years. As your rabbit gets older,
check that it is eating properly.
Let it sleep more if it wants to,
and help it to keep its fur clean.

As rabbits grow older,
their claws may grow
too long. A vet will
trim them for you.

Like people, rabbits grow old and
in time will die. If your rabbit is
very old or ill, it may be kinder to
let the vet put it to sleep.

You may feel sad when your pet
dies, but you will be able to look
back and remember all the happy
times you had together.

Words to Remember

bedding Hay and straw for a rabbit to sleep in.

groom To brush and comb an animal. Animals groom themselves with their teeth and tongue.

hutch The name of the home where a pet rabbit lives.

litter box A rabbit's toilet.

neutered A neutered animal has been operated on so that it cannot have babies.

run A long hutch made of wire and wood, where a rabbit can play outside.

suckling When a baby rabbit drinks its mother's milk, it is suckling.

vet A doctor for animals.

Rabbits Grow Fast

One week old.

Three weeks old.

Eight weeks old.

Index

Notes for Parents

A rabbit will give you and your family a great deal of pleasure, but it is a big responsibility. If you decide to buy a rabbit for your child, you will need to ensure that the animal is healthy, happy, and safe. You will also have to care for it if it is ill, and help your child with the animal's care until he or she is at least five years old. It will be your responsibility to make sure your child does not harm the rabbit and learns to handle it correctly.

Here are some other points to think about before you decide to own a rabbit:

- Some rabbits can be bad-tempered and can bite, kick, and scratch. Choose your rabbit carefully. Dwarf rabbits are easier for young children to look after.

- A rabbit can live for 12 years and costs money to feed and neuter. As it gets older, you may have to pay vet's bills.

- When your rabbit is a year old, you should take it to the vet. The vet can give it a shot to prevent serious diseases.

- When you go on vacation, you will need to make sure someone can care for your rabbit.

- Unless you are breeding rabbits, both males and females should be neutered.

- It is better to keep two rabbits together. Two females from the same litter are ideal, but males and females from the same litter can be kept together if the male is neutered. Two males from the same litter can be kept together, but they must be neutered to prevent them from fighting.

- If you have other pets, will the rabbit get along with them?

- Rabbits fed on the latest complete diets should not be fed mineral supplements unless the vet tells you to do this.

This book is only an introduction for young readers. If you have any questions about how to look after your pet rabbit, you can contact the Humane Society of the U.S., 2100 L Street NW, Washington, DC 20037.